A GUIDE TO IRISH MYTHOLOGY

First published in 2000 by
Mercier Press
PO Box 5 5 French Church St Cork
Tel: (021) 275040; Fax: (021) 274969; e.mail: books@mercier.ie
16 Hume Street Dublin 2
Tel: (01) 661 5299; Fax: (01) 661 8583; e.mail: books@marino.ie

Trade enquiries to CMD Distribution 55A Spruce Avenue
Stillorgan Industrial Park Blackrock County Dublin
Tel: (01) 294 2556; Fax: (01) 294 2564
e-mail: cmd@columba.ie

A CIP record for this book is available from the British Library.

ISBN 1 85635 305 2
10 9 8 7 6 5 4 3 2 1

Cover illustration and design by Penhouse Design
Printed by Cox & Wyman Ltd, Reading, Berks, UK

A GUIDE TO IRISH MYTHOLOGY

MAEVE WALSH

MERCIER PRESS

CONTENTS

INTRODUCTION

The early Irish did not acquire literacy until Christian times, maintaining their epic literature entirely by rote learning and transmission of the oral tradition. When the monastic scribes had fulfilled their sacred duty of copying the Scriptures they turned to more profane preoccupations and recorded nearly 1,000 years of this tradition in such books as *Lebor na hUidre* (*The Book of the Dun Cow*), the earliest extant manuscript written entirely in Irish, containing, among other epics, the *Táin Bó Cuailgne*, *Lebor na Nuachongbála* – later *Lebor Laignech* (*The Book of Leinster*) – and *Lebor Gabála Érenn* (*The Book of the Taking of Ireland*), which records the remembered history of the island from the foundation of the world.

Though entirely mythological in spirit, with many of the invaders assigned biblical forebears, folk memory and a certain amount of ancestor awe suggest that the invasions of Cesair, Partholón, the Firbolg, Nemed, the Tuatha Dé Danaan and the sons of Mil might have some historical basis. Milesius was also known as the *Míl Easpáin* ('Soldier of Spain'), a reasonable source of a Celtic invasion, a connection also indicated by the similarity of the Latin names *Iberia* and *Hibernia*. The Firbolg, it is suggested, may be connected with the Belgae, and the dreaded Fomorians, the personification of evil, were humanised as vicious sea pirates who came from the north.

Whatever about its source in the blurred area between history and folk memory, mythology served the same purpose for the Irish as for other races: it provided an explanation for the mysteries of life as experienced by an unlettered but far from primitive people. Meteorology, topography, the changing seasons, darkness and light, crop growth and failure, reproduction in animals and humans, birth, illness and death all needed to be accounted for. Immortal longings, wish-fulfilment, courage, magnanimity and a sense of greater predecessors demand some kind of objective correlative. As an island race, the Irish had to come to terms with the sea and try to explain its often terrifying changes; it was no wonder that they wished that their horses could ride on water and their boats require no human labour.

The early Irish were prone to local feuding and would have greatly wished to own magic weapons like the *gae-bolg* or have a champion like Cúchulainn to defend their *tuath*. Often, indeed, they would have been happy to have had the services of a near-invincible, quick-response police force like the *Fianna*. They were deft artificers and had great respect for the archaeological remains of their predecessors, investing the structures at Navan, the Boyne valley and Tara with numinous power. Feeling the need for a spiritual dimension to their cosmos, they devised a religion which would encompass the immaterial as well as the material. They typically assigned duties and responsibilities to particular deities, and, no doubt having pity for them sitting all ages lonesome on golden chairs, granted them the human delights of sports, music, feasting and lovemaking in their Otherworld.

This period's marvellous oral literature, whose

full richness can only be guessed at, was essentially the people's self-portrait, and the mythology it generated is one of the oldest, most lively and most consistent in Europe. It has obvious connections with those of the nearest Celtic countries to Ireland, Wales and Scotland. The linguistic differences between the Brythonic Welsh and the Goidelic vocabulary of Éire and Alba (Scotland) failed to disguise the similarities of, for example, Lir and Llyr, Lugh and Lleu, and Nuada and Lud. The essentially Welsh Arthurian cycle also has remarkable parallels in Irish mythology. Alba was regarded as almost an extension of Ulster, the narrow if stormy reach of the North Channel offering little hindrance to voyagers; in historical times the kingdom of Dál Riata straddled the two areas. Cúchulainn received his comprehensive education, including matchless military training, there, characteristically having several love affairs in the process and siring his only son, Conlaí. Deirdre and the sons of Usna fled for safety to Glen Etive in Argyll to avoid the wrath of Deirdre's betrothed, Conchobhar Mac Nessa.

The accumulated wealth of myth deals in the

main with gods and heroes, to use the title of Lady Gregory's popular book. Her first category includes mainly the Tuatha Dé Danaan, their enemies, the Fomorians, and their thralls, the Firbolg. Their hierarchy is somewhat like that of the Greek Olympians, with an awareness that there were also gods who made the gods, in Chesterton's phrase. The battles of the Olympians with the Titans find an echo in the struggles of the Dé Danaan with the Fomorians and, like their Greek and Roman counterparts, the early Irish had their *Götterdämmerung*: when worn out with internecine battle, they were assigned dwelling places in the Hollow Hills by the Dagda. They were happily amoral in the matter of sexuality among themselves and often found that they could not resist the sons and daughters of men, thereby producing a race of mortals who had special powers.

It is impossible now to estimate what stories were lost through the imperfect system of oral transmission and how many more disappeared in the destruction of manuscripts, which may have contained fuller accounts of Ireland's imagined past, in the centuries of the Viking raids. What remains is rich indeed, even if some of the cruder aspects of the pre-Christian tales would have suffered sanitisation at the hands of the monastic scribes. Stories tend to cluster round notable figures such as Cúchulainn, the 'Hound of Ulster', and Fionn Mac Cumhail and his band of superlative warriors, the *Fianna*. The earliest are those in which the invaders of the desirable island displace the inhabitants and are in turn displaced. The Irish pantheon thus established can stand comparison with those of Greek and Rome and some of the Irish stories have the added interest of the insistent intrusion of Christianity and history. These later tales mix the usual gods and heroes with saints and semi-mythical characters who may have been historical figures such as high kings. The gradual nature of the Christianisation of pagan Ireland meant that the oral tales which continued to be learned by heart and passed on had continual accretions, which involved the notable figures of the more recent past, the druids, the wonder-working holy men and the quasi-religious kings.

Important mythological characters may have several biographies with conflicting details, as in the case of Oisín, the poet-son of Fionn, who in one version is present at his son Oscar's interment and in another does not return to Ireland until 300 years after his hegira with Niamh Chinn Óir to the Land of Promise. Apart from the great figures that bestride the narrow world like the colossi they are, there are many minor characters with stories as fascinating as those in the greater epics. A great wealth of Irish myth and legend has been preserved in the manuscripts of the scholars and garnered from the *béaloideas* of the often-despised peasantry. It was the realisation of this fact that gave the Irish Literary Revival such strength and made writers like Yeats and Synge, prompted by Hyde and Gregory, opt for a native mythology rather than the classical one. A large portion of Yeats's turn-of-the-century poetry and much of his drama is steeped in these stories of the imagined Gaelic past. As a result, an educated Irish person would sooner admit to being ignorant of Zeus and Aphrodite than to being unaware of Aonghus Óg or Medb.

The purpose of this little book is to summarise the best-known and most important parts of the great store of Irish myths. The entries deal inevitably with the grander *personae* and the best-known versions of their stories. These are continually retold, especially for children, who are the best critics. Adults too can find great satisfaction in them, however. It is hardly surprising that these stories have continued to fascinate our writers, from Flann O'Brien to Seamus Heaney; our mythology best tells us what we are.

A

Aedh is the name of several characters in Irish mythology, most notably one of the four children of the sea god Lir* who were changed into swans by their stepmother Aoife*.

Áes ('people', *'aos'* in modern Irish) occurs in *Áes Sídhe*, 'the people of the hills', the old gods of Ireland, who were downgraded in later folklore to fairies and *Áes dána*, 'men of art'.

Aidín was the wife of Oscar*, grandson of Fionn Mac Cumhail*. She died of grief at Oscar's death and is buried in Beann Eadair (Howth).

Aileach was the Ulster fortress, traditionally built by the Tuatha Dé Danaan*, five miles northwest of Derry and the place where the goddesses Banba*, Fodla and Éire* divided the land of Ireland between them. Later it was a royal residence of the kings of Ulster and the seat of the Uí Néill in historical times. It was destroyed by the Munstermen in 1088 in retaliation for the Uí Néills' destruction of Kincora.

The marauders were supposed each to take a stone away with them so that the fortress might not be rebuilt, but the remains of the rebuilt circular cashel, which is more than a hundred feet in diameter and whose walls are thirteen feet thick, still stand.

Ailill is the name of several characters in Irish mythology, most notably Ailill, King of Connacht and pliable consort of Medb*, who drove him to invade Ulster and secure the Brown Bull of Cuailgne*. He was killed by Conall Cearnach* at Medb's instigation.

Áine is the Celtic sun goddess associated with Cnoc Áine in County Limerick. A fair, Aonach Áine, was held there each year at the beginning of harvest. She is sometimes identified, probably incorrectly, with Anú*, the mother of the gods.

Ainlé was the brother of Naoise* the lover of Deirdre*, and one of the three sons of Usna*.

Alba (also Albu and Albain) is Scotland, the home of the Picts.

Amergin (also Amairgen) was a poet, a warrior and one of the followers of Melesius*, the chief invader of Ireland.

Anú is the Irish mother goddess, cognate with Dana*.

Aobh was the mother of the pairs of twins Fionnuala* and Aedh* and Fiachra* and Conn* by the ocean god Lir*.

Aoibheall was the fairy queen associated with Craig Liath in County Clare and the presiding deity at Brian Merriman's *Cúirt an Meán-Oiche*.

Aoife was the younger sister of Aobh*. She became stepmother of the children of Lir* and turned them into swans. When Bodb Dearg*, her foster-father, discovered her crime he turned her into a demon of the air.

Aonghus Óg (also Angus and Oenghus) is the name of several characters in Irish mythology, most notably the Celtic god of love, the son of Dagda* and Boann*. He was the marriage-broker for Etáin* and Midir* and regularly came to the aid of his foster-son Diarmuid* and his lover Gráinne* in their flight from Gráinne's husband, Fionn Mac Cumhail*.

Árd Macha (Armagh) was the capital of Ulster. The city was associated with the triune goddess Macha* and chosen by St Patrick as the head-quarters of his church. It remains the primatial see.

Ardán was the son of Usna (see Deirdre).

Art was the son of Conn Cetcathach* and the father of Cormac Mac Art*. Art rejected the advances of his stepmother Bécuma*. She beat him at *fidchell*￼* with the help of spirits and was able to impose a Herculean task upon him: to find and rescue from her vicious parents the maiden Delbchaem, who was imprisoned behind a palisade, the pales of which were topped by the heads of suitors. He succeeded after many travails, beheading the parents and bringing Delbchaem back to Ireland. The evil Becuma was banished.

B

Balor (of the Evil Eye) was a death god and one of the Fomorians*. He had an eye the sight of which killed anyone who looked at it. It had been empowered by an accidental splash from a druidic draught of wisdom and required four men to lift the lid when its deadly power was needed in battle. In order to prevent the fulfilment of a prophesy that he would be slain by his own grandson he shut up his only daughter, Ethlinn*, in a glass tower on Tory Island*. Cian*, the son of the Dian Cécht*, seduced her, and their son Lugh Lámhfada* eventually killed Balor at one of the battles of Magh Tuireadh* (Moytura).

Banba is one of the three sister goddesses – the others being Fodla and Éire* – who each gave her name to Ireland.

Bean Sídhe ('banshee') means literally 'woman of the hills' and therefore 'fairy woman' after the degeneration of the ancient gods. Banshees became attached to individual families and warned them of approaching death by uttering an eldritch wail.

Bécuma is the goddess from Tír Tairnigiri* ('the Land of Promise'). She was banished after an affair with the son of Manannán Mac Lir to the human world, where she married Conn Cetcathach* in order to be near his son, Art*.

Beltaine (also Bealtaine) was the feast, held on May Eve, of the fires of Bel (or Bilé), a Celtic god of death, which marked the beginning of summer. This feast celebrated the sun's victory over the powers of darkness, and on that evening household fires were extinguished and rekindled by torches lit from the sun's rays by the local druids. Cattle were driven through bonfires as a symbol of purification and set free to graze the new grass.

Blathnát (also Blanaid, 'little flower') loved Cúchulainn* but was carried off by Cú Roi, Cúchulainn's patron, as his wife. Cúchulainn went to rescue her but Cú Roi's Munster fort lacked an obvious entrance. The resourceful Blathnát emptied milk into an inner stream, revealing the location of the portal as it seeped out, and the attack was successful: she was rescued and Cú Roi slain. Among the prisoners was Cú Roi's bard Fercherdne, who, in revenge for his master's death, later seized Blathnát and jumped with her over a cliff on the Beara peninsula.

Boann (also Board) is the goddess associated with the source of the River Boyne. She bore Aonghus Óg*, the love god, to the Dagda* after her husband, Elcmar, was sent by him on an errand which seemed to last a day but in fact took nine months. She refused to honour the *geis** associated with the Well of Knowledge and was drowned when the water from the well pursued her, forming the river.

Bodb Dearg was the son of the Dagda* and the deity of Connacht. He succeeded his father as ruler of the Tuatha Dé Danaan*. His daughter Sadb* was the mother of Oisín*, the son of Fionn Mac Cumhail*.

Bran is the hero of the voyage tale *Immram Brain*. In this tale he met Manannán Mac Lir* and, because of the aeons spent in the Land of Women (which he and his crew experienced as a single year), was condemned to wander forever; to touch the land of Ireland would have reduced him to his human age. He was the son of Febal, who is associated with Lough Foyle in Ulster. Bran was also the name of the chief hound of Fionn Mac Cumhail* – his nephew. Fionn's sister Tuireann had been changed into a bitch and gave birth to

Bran and Sceolan*. Fionn had to kill Bran when he attacked Sadb*, the mother of Oisín*; Sadb was at the time in the form of a fawn.

Breasal was the High King of the World for the Celts. He gave his name to Hy-Brasil*, the Irish Atlantis, which spelt death to anyone who saw it on one of its septennial appearances.

Bricriu was Nemthenga ('poisoned tongue'), the chief troublemaker at the court of Conchobhar* at Emain Macha*. At a feast, he caused strife between Cúchulainn* and the other Red Branch warriors over who should have the hero's portion. The account of his mischief-making is described in the tale Fled Bricenn ('Bricriu's Feast'). Asked to adjudicate between the Brown Bull of Cuailgne and the White Bull of Connacht, he was trampled to death by the fighting animals.

Brigid (also Brigit) is the triune goddess and daughter of the Dagda*. Her cult was later subsumed into that of St Brigid, for whom a perpetual fire was maintained at her Kildare shrine until the Reformation. Her feast day, 1 February, is also Imbolg*, the beginning of the Celtic spring.

Bruigh na Bóinne is the palace of the Boyne identified as Newgrange, home of Aonghus Óg*.

C

Cailleach Beara is the mountain goddess associated with the border peninsula of Kerry and Cork. She outlived seven periods of fertility and seven husbands who died of old age; she thus became synonymous with longevity.

Cairbre was the son of Cormac Mac Art*. He brought about the destruction of the *Fianna*.

Cairbre Caitcheann ('cat-head') was so called because he had the ears of a cat. He reigned at the time of the Milesians over a land stricken with sterility.

Caoilte ('the slender man') was the fleetest of foot among the *Fianna* and its leading poet. He is said to have returned from the Otherworld* to relate to St Patrick the adventures of the brotherhood.

Cathbad was a druid associated with the court of Conchobhar* and the grandfather of Cúchulainn*. He prophesied the latter's short but glorious career and the fate of Deirdre*.

Cesair (also Cessair) was the granddaughter of Noah and the wife of Fintan*. Cesair, denied entrance to the Ark, built a ship and after seven years reached the shores of Ireland and became the first settler. Abandoned by Fintan, she died of grief just before the Flood.

Cet was a warrior from Connacht. He was active in the war with the men of Ulster and drove the 'brain ball' into the forehead of Conchobhar*, causing his death seven years later. He stole the lethal device, which was made from the brains of Mac Da Thó* mixed with lime, from its manufacturer, Conall Cearnach*.

Cian was the son of Dian Cecht* and the god of medicine. He dressed as a woman to make his way to Tory Island* to recover his cow, the Glas Gaibhleann, which had been stolen by Balor*, and seduced Ethlinn*, Balor's daughter, in spite of her imprisonment in a crystal tower. Their child was Lugh Lámhfada*. Cian was eventually slain by the sons of Tuireann* in spite of turning himself into a hare.

An Claideamh Soluis: was 'the sword of light'. The sword was invincible in the hands of Nuada*. It was chosen by the Gaelic League as the title of its newspaper, which succeeded *Fáinne an Lae* and was published between 1899 and 1930.

Cliodhna was the goddess of beauty. She lived in Tír Tairnigiri* ('the Land of Promise') and fell in love with a mortal, Ciabhán of the Curling Locks. They escaped to Glandore in County Cork and lived happily on the shore until, at her father's instruction, Manannán Mac Lir* sent a huge wave, which carried her back home and left her lover grieving.

Conall Cearnach ('victorious') was the cousin and foster-brother of Cúchulainn*. He was the chief warrior of the Red Branch* until the coming of Cúchulainn. He avenged Cúchulainn's death and devised the 'brain ball' that Cet* used to begin the destruction of Conchobhar*.

Conan Maol ('bald') was one of the two sons of Morna. He appears as a boastful and foul-mouthed clown in the stories of the *Fianna**, especially in the episode of the Giolla Deacair. His abilities as a warrior, however, were never in question.

Conchobhar Mac Nessa was the King of Ulster. His territory was defended by the knights of the Red Branch*. He was the son of Fachtna Fathach,

King of Ulster, and Nessa*, who married the new king, Fergus Mac Roth*, on his father's death. From him she obtained the right for Conchobhar to be king for a year and he proved so popular a ruler that he was confirmed on the throne. He married Medb* of Connacht, who left him for Ailill*. His tragic and treacherous love of Deirdre*, who preferred to die rather than marry him, is the basis of one of the best-known Irish stories. He died seven years after being struck by the 'brain ball' used by Cet*; he was warned that this brain ball would prove lethal should he ever ride a horse or get in a rage. One late version of his story has him born on the same day as Christ and another tells of his death on hearing of the Crucifixion.

Conlaí was the son of Cúchulainn* and Aoife. He was killed by his father, with whom he engaged in single combat.

Conn Cetcathach ('of the hundred battles') is a mainly mythical character who has some basis in historical fact as a second-century high king whose second wife, Becuma, married him only because she lusted after his son Art*. In one story he sees in a vision a woman representing sovereignty who with Lugh* lists his descendants who will reign in Ireland. Conn was also the name of one of the children of Lir*.

Cormac Mac Art was a high king who may have reigned in the third century and about whom many myths accreted. He was the patron of the *Fianna** and father of Gráinne. While trying to defend his son Cellach he lost an eye and so had to relinquish the throne to his son Cairbre*.

Craiftine was the harpist of Labraid Loinseach*. His music lulled the parents of the Gaulish princess Moriath to sleep so that Labraid and she could make love. He used the same means to render Labraid's enemies ineffective.

Crane Bag was a bag made from the skin of a nymph called Aoife who was killed when she was turned into a crane by Manannán Mac Lir*, the father of her lover. The bag was a source of magical articles; it was empty at low tide and full only at high tide.

Cromm Cruach was the gold idol, with 'sub-gods twelve', to whom first fruits and human sacrifices were offered. It stood in Magh Sclecht, the 'plane of adoration' in Cavan. It bent over St Patrick in a threatening manner but then sank back, overcome by the saint's sanctity.

Cromm Dubh was the idol worshipped in Connacht and Munster and associated with Fraughan Sunday*, which until recently was known locally as *Domnach Chrom Dubh*.

Cuailgne is the modern Cooley peninsula in County Louth, home of the Brown Bull of Daire*, which was the subject of the epic *Táin Bó Cuailgne**.

Cúchulainn ('the Hound of Culann') was the Hound of Ulster. He was the greatest of the epic heroes of Irish mythology and the protagonist of many wondrous tales and amorous adventures. On the eve of her wedding to Sualtaim Mac Roth, his mother, Dechtire, was spirited away to the Otherworld*, from which she returned with a baby boy named Sétanta*, whose father was Lugh Lámhfada*. Even as a child his feats of strength and athleticism were notable; he was able to run fast enough to catch a ball that he had hit with his own hurley stick – hence the number of modern Setanta golf courses – and leap high in the air like a salmon. The boy's adult name resulted from his killing of Culann (who may have been Manannán Mac Lir*), the hound of the smith of Conchobhar*, and his agreeing to serve as guard dog until a suitable replacement could be found.

His capacity as a warrior – he was the chief of Conchobhar's Red Branch Knights* – was increased by the *gae-bolg**, the war spear of his Scottish female tutor Scáthach, his sword Cailid-cheann ('hard-headed') and his self-induced battle-frenzy, recovery from which required immersion in three tubs of ice-cold water and, once, a parade of naked women led out from Emain Macha* by Conchobhar's wife. His greatest feat was his single-handed defence of Ulster against the Connacht warriors of Medb* and Ailill*, during which he was constrained to kill his best friend, Ferdia*, at the fierce Battle of the Ford. His enemy, the Mórrígán, whose love he had rejected, perched on his shoulder in the customary form of a crow to show he was near death, his judgement distracted by the phantom army sent against him by the daughters of Calatin, whom he had killed. He finally capitulated to hunger, loss of blood from the wounds inflicted by Ferdia and the magic of Medb and her minions. (This final stance is the theme of Oliver Sheppard's famous 1916 sculpture in the General Post Office in Dublin.)

The two main women in Cúchulainn's life were his wife, Emer*, and Fand*, the wife of Manannán Mac Lir*, but his only son, Conlaí*, was born of Aoife, the sister of his tutor Scáhach. Associated with the hero is his charioteer Laeg, who drove the magic horses the Liath Macha and the Dubh Sanglainn and saved his master's life by stepping between him and a spear thrown by Lugaid, the son of Cú Roí, King of Munster, whom Cúchulainn had earlier slain.

D

The Dagda was the head of the Tuatha Dé Danaan*, the son of the earth goddess Dana and the father of the Irish gods. He possessed a magic harp which could produce the three types of music: *goltraí*, *geantraí* and *suantraí*, inducing sorrow, laughter and sleep, respectively, the last virtue helping him to subdue his main adversaries, the Fomorians*. In some of the stories he seems to degenerate into a buffoon, appearing as a fat old man at the second battle of Magh Tuireadh* but possessing a magic cauldron of food and drink. After the occlusion of the Tuatha Dé Danaan he allotted a portion of Ireland to each deity, reserving Bruigh na Boinne* for himself, but was tricked out of possession of it by his son Aonghus Óg*.

Dana (also Danu) was the ancient mother goddess from whom the Tuatha Dé Danaan took their name. She was the mother of the Dagda by Bilé, a god of death.

The Dark Druid: (also *Fer Doireach*) was the black magician who changed Sadb*, the daughter of the Bodb Dearg*, into the shape of a fawn.

Dechtiré (also Dectera) was the daughter of the druid Cathbad*, the granddaughter of Aonghus Óg* and the mother of Cúchulainn*. She was taken away with fifty handmaidens by Lugh Lámhfada on the eve of her wedding to Sualtaim Mac Roth. She appeared at the Boyne three years later with a newborn son, Sétanta*, who was accepted by Sualtaim as his son. Sétanta grew up to be Cúchulainn. The fact that the hero was not born in Ulster enabled him to withstand the curse of Macha*, which enfeebled the men of that province during the war with Medb*.

Deirdre (also Deirdru) was the tragic heroine known as Deirdre of the Sorrows and daughter of Felim Mac Dall, an Ulster chieftain. It was foretold by Cathbad* that she was destined to be the fairest of women and that she would marry a king but bring nothing but misery upon Ulster. The warriors of Conchobhar Mac Nessa* wanted to kill the child but the king insisted that she be spared and reared to be his queen.

She was placed in the nursing charge of Lebarcham*, who became her confidante as she grew up. One winter day as they watched ravens tearing at a lamb's carcass she vowed to love a man whose skin would be as white as snow, whose hair would be like the raven's wing and whose lips would be as red as blood. When she eventually saw from the battlements of Emain Macha* the warrior Naoise*, the eldest of the sons of Usna*, who fulfilled all these criteria, she was lost. She fled with him and his brothers Ainlé* and Ardán* to Glen Etive in Alba*, where they had a period of happiness before returning to Ireland under the safe conduct of Fergus Mac Roth*. The brothers were treacherously killed and Deirdre, after a year's silence in Conchobhar's house, was given as wife to Eoghan Mac Durthacht, who had slain Naoise. On her way to Eoghan's house she threw herself from the chariot, dashing her brains out against a rock. She is the Celtic equivalent of Helen of Troy and a symbol of dissolution.

Dian Cecht was the god of medicine. He fashioned a silver hand to replace the one Nuada had lost at the battle of Magh Tuireadh*.

Although he was known as Airgetlámh, the defect precluded his kingship until Dian Cecht's son Miach*, who was a more cunning artificer than him, provided him with a hand of flesh and blood. As a consequence Miach was killed in a fit of jealousy by his father.

Diarmuid is the name of several characters in Irish mythology, most notably Diarmuid Ua Duibhne, 'Diarmuid of the Love Spot', which was placed on him by the goddess of youth, making him irresistible to women. He was taken when still a child to be fostered by Aonghus Óg*. His father, discovering that his wife had borne a child to Aonghus's steward Roc, crushed the infant. Roc restored him to life in the form of a giant boar that bided its time in the thickets of Ben Bulben as Diarmuid's nemesis. Diarmuid grew up to be a beautiful youth and a leading warrior in the *Fianna*, which was led by his ageing uncle Fionn Mac Cumhail*.

Fionn became betrothed to Gráinne*, the daughter of Cormac Mac Art*. Gráinne had no wish to marry an old man and tried to seduce Fionn's son Oisín*; having failed in this, she placed Diarmuid under *geis** to love her. Unable to break the obligation, he eloped with her from Cormac's palace at Tara*, pursued by the *Fianna*. At the beginning of the relationship he treated her as a sister, taking care to inform Fionn of this restraint, but he eventually allowed himself to be seduced and for sixteen years they were pursued throughout Ireland. (Some of the places where they concealed themselves, as far apart as Donegal and Kerry, are still known as Dermot and Grania's Beds.) Eventually Diarmuid's foster-father, Aonghus*, arranged a cessation of hostilities and the couple settled down to a tranquil life and had four sons and a daughter.

Gráinne insisted upon the overt respectability of visits from her father and Fionn, and after a year of feasting Diarmuid was persuaded to go with the *Fianna* on a boar-hunt in the woods near Ben Bulben. The quarry, Diarmuid's metamorphosed half-brother, became their pursuer and mortally wounded him. As he lay dying Fionn refused to bring him the water which in his hands would restore life. When Oscar, Fionn's own grandson, threatened to kill the chief if he did not bring the water, he complied – but allowed the liquid to trickle through his fingers. Aonghus and the sorrowing Gráinne brought the body to Bruigh na Boinne*. The parallels with the Arthurian triangles of Arthur, Guinevere and Lancelot and Mark, Isolde and Tristan are striking.

Donn Cuailgne is the Brown Bull of Cooley. Originally a herd of the Bodb Dearg*, called Nár, he carried on a bloody conflict with Friuch, the herd of Ochall of Connacht, until, after many incarnations, both became bulls, Friuch ending as Finnbhenach*, the White Bull of Connacht. At the end of the *Táin** war they fought and killed each other.

The Druids were a historical, quasi-religious class, both male and female, who were the educated elite of Celtic society. The historical Druids' knowledge of philosophy, history, medicine, law and natural science meant that they were regarded with awe and some terror, and Patrician Christianity was characterised by accommodation with these mages. In myth they appear as wizards.

E

Éire (also Eriu) was the Dé Danaan goddess who gave Ireland its most customary name, though the names of her sisters Fodla and Banba are used poetically. They welcomed the Milesians* to Ireland, each trying to prevail upon the invaders to name the country after her. Amergin* finally made the decision as to the country's name.

Emain Macha was the seat of the Ulster kings and, after Tara*, the best-known Irish royal enclosure. It is likely to have been sited at Navan (*'n Emhain'*) near Armagh City, which shares the element *'Macha'* in its name and where striking archeological remains are to be seen. Many of the e*achtraí* of the Red Branch Cycle took place in or near the enclosure. It was said to consist of three richly appointed chambers, the Craobh Ruadh, the Craobh Dearg and the Teite Brecc ('speckled house'): the first, which named the cycle, was the feasting and sleeping quarters of the king and his warriors, the second was the treasury and the last was the armoury. Its resemblance to Arthur's Camelot is striking. Its regal history lasted 600 years and it was the appropriate choice for St Patrick's ecclesiastical capital.

Emer was the wife of Cúchulainn*. She possessed the 'six gifts of womenhood': beauty, chastity, sweet speech, needlework, voice and wisdom. Cúchulainn fell in love with her when he was very young but her father Forgall was not in favour of their marriage and sent him to Alba* to train as a warrior. On his return Cúchulainn took Emer by force, killing many of Forgall's warriors and causing Forgall to commit suicide. The couple's relationship was stormy, though their love was never in doubt. Cúchulainn, as befitted a demigod, was loved by many women and happily returned their interest. When he fell in love with Fand* the two women settled matters peaceably between them, Fand returning to her husband Manannán Mac Lir*. Just before his last battle Cúchulainn had a prophetic vision of Emain Macha* in flames and Emer's body being thrown over the palisade. She fell dead into her husband's grave after uttering a famous keen over his remains.

Étain is the name of several characters in Irish mythlogy, most notably the beautiful wife of the god Midir*. She figures in a complicated and sophisticated tale of many reincarnations. She was released by her father Ailill to the marriage broker Aonghus Óg* only after he had performed three formidable tasks. She suffered the envy of Midir's first wife, Fuamnach*, who changed her by turns into a pool of water, a worm and a fly to confuse Midir as he searched for her. Eventually he recognised her in the form of a fly which never left his presence. Fuamnach then caused a magic wind to blow; this tossed the fly about the sky for seven years until it made its way to Bruigh na Boinne*, home of Aonghus Óg*. He told Midir, but Fuamnach, hearing the news, called up another seven-year wind. Finally the fly was swallowed by the pregnant wife of Etar* and the resulting daughter, also called Étain, was an avatar of the original but was unaware of her previous history. When she grew up, Midir tried to claim her as his wife but yielded her to her husband, Eochaidh, to whom she bore another Étain.

Etar was the Ulster warrior of Conchobhar Mac Nessa*. Etar's pregnant wife swallowed Étaín* in the shape of fly and produced a mortal daughter, a second Étaín, whom Midir* tried to claim as his lost spouse.

Ethlinn (also Ethniu, Eithne) was the daughter of Balor of the Evil Eye*. Balor kept her from the sight of men shut up in a crystal tower on Tory Island* because of a prophecy that he would be slain by his grandchild. Balor stole the Glas Gaibhleann*, a cow that Cian*, the son of the Dian Cecht*, was tending. Cian sought help from a druidess called Birog who enabled him, dressed as a woman, to penetrate Ethlinn's tower and make love to her while her female guardians slept. Having retrieved the cow, Birog and Cian returned to the mainland, leaving Ethlinn pregnant. She had three children, one of whom escaped the drowning imposed by Balor. He was fostered by the sea god Manannán Mac Lir*, called Lugh Lámhfhada*, and became the god of arts and crafts. Ethlinn eventually married Nuada Airgetlámh* and became an ancestor of Fionn Mac Cumhail*.

F

Fand was the wife of Manannán Mac Lir* and the mistress of Cúchulainn*. During a period of estrangement from her husband when her home in Tír Tairnigiri* ('the Land of Promise') was attacked by the Fomorians*, she sent for Cúchulainn to defend her, offering him her bed in payment. He was successful and stayed for a month, arranging to meet Fand again on the Yew Tree strand in the Cooley peninsula in County Louth. His wife, Emer*, found out and resolved to kill Fand but, finding that the goddess genuinely loved her husband, agreed to relinquish him. Manannán arrived and demanded that Fand choose between him and the mortal. She returned with her husband to the Otherworld, deciding that if she had gone with Cúchulainn he would have no mate worthy of him, whereas the hero still had Emer. Manannán shook his cloak between the lovers so that they could never meet again and the mortals were granted the gift of forgetfulness.

Ferdia (also Ferdiad) was a fellow student and the closest friend of Cúchulainn; the two were trained together in Alba* by Scáthach*. During the war of the *Táin** he took the side of Connacht and, though he tried to avoid conflict with his friend, was goaded into combat by the malevolent Medb*. He was killed on the fourth day because Cúchulainn made use of the gae-*bolg**. The effect of his friend's death on Cúchulainn was so dispiriting that all the fighting spirit left him and he died shortly afterwards.

Fergus is the name of several characters in Irish mythlogy, most notably Fergus Mac Roth, who acquiesced in the wish of his wife, Nessa*, that her son Conchobhar* should reign in Emain Macha* for a year. In fact Conchobhar refused to give up the throne but Fergus still served him as emissary to Naoise* and Deirdre* in Alba*. When he learned of Conchobhar's treachery he joined with Medb* and Ailill* in Connacht and fought the Ulstermen during the Táin war. He was traditionally a scholar and set down in Ogam the account of the fighting. He was killed by a spear thrown by Ailill*, who had found him swimming with Medb.

Fiachra was the son of Lir*. He and his sister Fionnuala* and brothers Aedh* and Conn* were changed into swans by their stepmother Aoife*. **The *Fianna*** was the band of warriors (with ancillary physicians, poets, musicians and druids) whose task was to guard the High King of Ireland. The *Fianna* were said to have been founded in 300 BC; their detailed adventures recounted in the Ossianic Cycle* probably spring from a euhemerist memory of a historical military elite. It was extremely difficult to qualify for membership: almost-superhuman feats of memory, athleticism and courage were required. The most famous leader of the *Fianna* was Fionn Mac Cumhail*, who, with his son Oisín* and brother warriors, guarded Cormac Mac Art*. The word *'fianna'* means 'warrior-hunters' and was used in Fianna Éireann (Countess Markievicz's revolutionary band of boy scouts) and in the name of the modern political party Fianna Fáil ('soldiers of destiny'). The nineteenth-century insurrectionist Fenian movement also took its name from the cycle.

Fidchell is an ancient Irish board game analogous to chess which is mentioned in many tales and sagas. Mastery in the game was a requirement for both deities and heroes.

Finnbhenach was the White-Horned Bull of Connacht and the adversary of Donn Cuailgne*. Originally a herd called Friuch, at his metamorphosis he refused to become part of the stock of Medb* and joined that of Ailill* instead, thus precipitating the war of the *Táin**.

Fintan was the husband of Cesair*. He survived the Flood by taking the form of a salmon. He ate the Nuts of Knowledge before going to live in a pool in the Boyne and was greatly sought as the Salmon of Knowledge.

Fionn Mac Cumhail is the most celebrated of the Irish heroes, outdoing even Cúchulainn* in fame. He was the son of Cumal, a leader of the *Fianna**, and Murna of the White Neck* and was given the name Demna. Cumal was killed by Goll Mac Morna* because of his elopement with Fionn's mother, who was of the same clan, and during most of his childhood the boy was at risk from Goll, who had become the leader of the *Fianna**. He established his reputation as a warrior early, slaying Lia* and recovering the Crane Bag*. He was sent for education to the druid Finegas, who lived beside the Boyne and hoped some day to hook Fintan*, the Salmon of Knowledge. The day he succeeded, he gave the fish to Demna to cook and the boy, burning his thumb, sucked it to ease the pain and stored Fintan's knowledge in a tooth, known in later stories as *fiacail feasa Fionn* ('Fionn's tooth of wisdom').

Now known as Fionn ('the fair one') and equipped with his father's magic spear, he defended Tara* from an attack by a demon and was made head of the *Fianna** by Cormac Mac Art*. For many years he led the *Fianna* in their golden age, now faithfully served by Goll Mac Morna*, Diarmuid Ua Duibhne* and his son Oisín*, whose mother was the goddess Sadb*. His hounds Bran* and Sceolan* were actually his nephews, the offspring of his bewitched sister Tuireann.

He had many amorous adventures but the story of his betrothal in his old age to Gráinne*, the daughter of Cormac Mac Art*, and her elopement with his close friend Diarmuid* is the best-known and most dramatic episode in the sequence. Like Arthur of Camelot, whose life has many parallels to his, he is thought not to have died but to have remained in a twilight sleep with the rest of the *Fianna*, waiting for the call that will wake him in Ireland's hour of greatest need.

Fingal (of the cave in Mendelssohn's Hebridean Isle of Staffa) is identified with him, and in later Ulster mythology he is the giant builder of the basaltic Giant's Causeway in County Antrim – an attempt to construct a path to Alba so that he could fight with an equivalent giant on the other side of the Sea of Moyle. The same story has him scooping up a piece of land from the centre of Ulster and tossing it at his rival, creating in an instant the Isle of Man and Lough Neagh. The Causeway's Irish name, *Clochán na bhFomaraigh* ('the stepping stones of the Fomorians') suggests earlier builders.

Fionnuala was the daughter of Lir*. She and her brothers Aedh*, Conn* and Fiachra* were changed into swans by Aoife*, their stepmother and aunt. They languished for 500 years on the western ocean, for 500 more on the Sea of Moyle* and for a further 500 on Lough Derravaragh in Westmeath. By then, as the later stories tell, Christianity had come to Ireland and the sound of a monastery bell restored them to (aged) human form and gave them time to be baptised before their simultaneous deaths.

Firbolg ('bag-men') were early inhabitants of Ireland who were enslaved by the Tuatha Dé Danaan* and made to carry fertile earth to the rocky parts of the terrain. Historically they were pre-Celtic inhabitants, with notable differences in stature and physiognomy from the tall, sandy-haired Celts.

Fomorians were a grotesque (often with single arms, legs and eyes) and malignant people, the dark and evil forces of Irish myth. They lived mostly on Tory Island* but, as their name suggests, could exist under the sea. Balor* is their best-known leader. Their power was finally broken at the second battle of Magh Tuireadh*.

Fuamnach was the first wife of Midir*. In her jealousy she caused Étain*, Midir's second wife, great turmoil. She was killed by Aonghus Óg*, who brought her head as a trophy to Brúigh na Boinne*.

G

Gae-Bolg ('belly-spear') was the magic spear of Cúchulainn*. It had one entry wound but thirty barbs which opened inside the body. It was given to Cúchulainn by his tutor and lover, Scáthach*, who taught him to throw it using his foot.

Geis was a taboo or imposition used by the Druids* which required obedience when placed upon someone. It was an unusually effective control: disobedience to it, which was largely unthinkable, would have meant social ostracism and inevitable and painful death. The *geis* put upon Diarmuid* by Gráinne* (with the help of her druid Daire) led to his elopement with her.

Glas Gaibhleann (also Gaibhneann) was the magic grey cow owned by Cian* which was stolen by Balor* and taken to Tory Island*. In pursuit of this cow, Cian met Balor's daughter Ethlinn* and sired Lugh Lámhfada*, who would fulfil the prophecy about Balor's death.

Goll Mac Morna was the leader of the *Fianna**
before Fionn Mac Cumhail*, slayed Fionn's
father, Cumall, and was the relentless enemy of
Fionn. On Fionn's majority, however, Goll
became his most loyal follower and married his
daughter Cebha. Later he killed Fionn's son
Cairell, and when Oscar*, Fionn's grandson,
tried to settle the matter, Goll threw a spear at
him. Trapped by his late comrades, he starved
to death after twelve days.

Gráinne is the Guinevere of Irish myth. She was
the daughter of Cormac Mac Art*, who was
betrothed to Fionn Mac Cumhail* in old age.
Seeing her future husband, she immediately turned
her attention to his son Oisín* as a more appropriate
mate. Rejected by him, she put Diarmuid Ua
Duibhne* under *geis** to run away with her. The
many 'beds' throughout Ireland associated with
the runaways are an indication of the fulfilment of
Fionn's curse that they would not sleep in the same
bed on consecutive nights. After Diarmuid's death
she returned with Fionn to Tara*, where she
suffered the continuing obloquy of the Fianna*.
Her name signifies ugliness and she is always seen
as a spoiled and wilful woman.

H

Hy-Brasil (also Ó Brasil) was the land of Breasal, called High King of the World. The *'Hy'* is the Irish *'í'* ('island') and in later folklore refers to an Irish Atlantis, a refuge for some of the Tuatha Dé Danaan* after their defeat by the sons of Mil*. It appeared to the west of the Aran Islands once in seven years and spelt death to anyone who saw it. It was regarded as an earthly paradise; in the words of Gerald Griffin's poem:

> *Men thought it a region of sunshine and rest*
> *And they called it Hy-Brasail, the isle of the*
> *blest.*

The name was internationally known and the place was marked on old charts: when the fifteenth-century Iberian explorers found South America they called the most easterly region Brazil.

I

Imbolg was the spring festival associated with the deity Brigid*. It was celebrated on 1 February, the feast day of the Christian saint Brigid, who may have been a priestess of the goddess.

Immram was a mythological wonder voyage, such as that of Mael Dúin and the Christian epic *Navigation Brendani*.

Iseult (also Isolde) was the Irish princess in the Arthurian cycle who, betrothed to King Mark of Cornwall, fell in love with Tristan, the king's nephew, who was sent to fetch her from Ireland. She gave her name to the County Dublin village of Chapelizod.

Isle of Man is *'Ellan Vannin'* in Manx and *'Oileán Mhanannán'* ('Manannán's Isle') in the original Irish. The island, which is roughly equidistant from Ireland, England, Scotland and Wales, figures little in early mythology apart from the belief that the mist and rain that blankets it from time to time is generated by

Manannán Mac Lir* as a protection against
enemies. It was probably British rather than
Irish until the fourth century AD but colonisation
from Ireland made the language of its people
clearly Gaelic. In later folk tales it was formed
by the land scooped out from mid-Ulster that
the giant (loosely associated with Fionn Mac
Cumhail) who made the Antrim Causeway used
as a missile against the Scottish giant Fingal,
thus simultaneously forming Lough Neagh.

L

Labraid Loinseach was the son of Ailill Áine,
King of Leinster. He was poisoned by his uncle
Cobhthach, who afterwards forced the boy to
eat his father's heart. The trauma rendered him
dumb and he remained silent during a sojourn
in Britain and Gaul to escape the machinations
of the same great-uncle. He recovered his voice
after being hit by a hurley stick in a game.
While in Gaul he fell in love with Moriath, the
daughter of Scoriath, the king of Fir Morc, but
her mother guarded her night and day, sleeping
with one eye open. The girl taught Craiftine*,
Labraid's harpist, a magic tune that sent her
mother and father to sleep, and the couple were
able to make love. The parents accepted the *fait
accompli* and Scoriath fitted out Labraid with an
army to invade Leinster and defeat his great-
uncle. Cobhthach was lulled into a false sense
of security when he heard that the captain of the
Gaulish army could not speak. Craiftine played

his sleep music and Cobhthach's army was easily defeated and its leader and thirty bodyguards burned to death in their stronghold.

In a more famous story Labraid was said to have horse's ears, a blemish which, if discovered, would have rendered him incapable of kingship. Each barber who cut his hair was killed in order to keep the king's defect a secret. Once, however, the king, heeding the prayers of a barber's mother, spared him after he swore that he would remain silent about the defect. The barber, unable to keep the secret to himself, told a tree, which in time was cut down to make Craftine a new harp. When the harp was played it revealed the king's secret.

Lebor Gabála (*The Book of the Takings*) is a twelfth-century chronicle detailing the history of Ireland from the Creation until the time of the book's compilation. It describes the early waves of immigrants who colonised Ireland, including Cesair*, Partholón*, Nemed*, the Firbolg*, the Tuatha Dé Danaan* and finally the Milesians* (the historical Gaels).

Lebarcham was a poet and the nurse of Deirdre*. She tried to persuade Conchobhar Mac Nessa* that her ward's striking beauty had faded during her sojourn with Naoise* in Alba*. One of Conchobhar's spies reported that Deirdre was as beautiful as ever and the tragic events were set in train.

Lia Fáil ('Stone of Destiny') was the crowning stone for Irish high kings at Tara. It crowed with pleasure at the touch of a rightful king. Some say it was this stone that was taken to Scone near Perth and used at the coronation of Dál Riata kings. The Stone of Scone was later removed to Westminster Abbey by Edward I of England (1239–1307) and used at coronations there. It was stolen by Scottish students in 1950 and recovered in 1952. It was finally returned to Scotland in 1998.

Lir is the ocean god whose name was immortalised by Shakespeare as the ancient King Lear of Britain. In Irish mythology his fame stems from his children, Fionnuala* and her brothers. One of these brothers was Manannán*, who replaced Lir as the Irish Poseidon.

Lugh was one of the greatest of the Irish gods and was known as Lámhfada ('long-handed'). A sun god and patron of art and craft, he was the grandson and slayer of Balor* (at the second battle of Magh Tuireadh*) and was fostered by Manannán Mac Lir*. He came to the court of Nuada of the Silver Hand*, who was the chief god of the Tuatha Dé Danaan*, and was allowed to rule the other deities for thirteen days. The father of Cúchulainn* by the mortal Dechtiré*, he fought by the Ulster hero's side when he had grown weak from hunger and the wounds inflicted by Ferdia*. His name is found in the Celtic name for London, Lugdunum, and in such place names as Lyons and Leiden.

Lughnasa was the harvest festival incorporating the name of the god Lugh* and marking the beginning of autumn. It was a first-fruits rite marked by sacred games and survives in the modern *Lúnasa* (the month of August). It is cognate with the English festival of Lammas, which also began on 1 August.

M

Macha was a goddess who appears in several
incarnations: as a war goddess, another name for
the Mórrígán*, the wife of Nemed*, the mysterious wife of Crunniuc Mac Agnomian, the builder
of Emain Macha* and the founder of the first
hospital in Ireland, a deed commemorated by a
sculpture at the Northwest Hospital at Altna-
gelvin in Derry.

Cruinniuc was an Ulster chieftain who, after
being widowed, took in a mysterious visitor
called Macha and made her his second wife.
When pregnant with twins (the significance of
the word *'emain'*) she was made to race against
the king's horses because of an unfortunate
boast of her husband. She won the race but died
giving birth at Emain Macha; her curse condemned all Ulster males for eighty-one gener-
ations to suffer the pangs of childbirth for five
days and four nights at the time of Ulster's
greatest need. As a result of this curse Cú-

chulainn, not being of Ulster birth, was alone able to fight the forces of Connacht during the *Táin* war.

Macha Mong Ruadh ('Red-Haired Macha'), then high queen, is credited with the building of Navan Fort*, in 337 BC, and Árd Macha.
Mael Dúin is the hero of the fabulous *Immram* Curaig Maile Dúin*, which was the source for Tennyson's *Voyage of Maeldune* (1880) and inspired the medieval *Navigatio Brendani*. Mael Dúin was the son of a raped nun who died in childbirth. His father was from Aran and died at the hands of sea raiders. When Mael Dúin became a man he gathered round him sixty Irish warriors and with them set sail to find his father's murderers. During this Irish odyssey, done in a currach made of skin, they visited thirty-three islands, each of which was filled with wonders of different kinds: giant ants, demon horses, talking birds, intoxicating fruit, protective walls of flame and a lake whose waters had the capacity to restore youth. Most popular with his band was *Tír na mBan* ('the Land of Women'), which was ruled by a queen where a partner was provided for every man and

there was an endless supply of food, drink and entertainment. Eventually the mortals grew tired of timeless beauty and sailed for home. When they finally found their quarry, instead of killing them they made peace.

Magh Tuireadh ('the Plain of Towers', also Moytura) is the site of two famous battles, the first near Cong in County Mayo between the native Firbolg* and the Dé Danaan*, led by Nuada*, the second in north Sligo between the Dé Danaan and the Fomorians*; Nuada was slain by Balor* in this battle.

Manannán Mac Lir was the chief god of the sea. He had the ability to drive his chariot over the waves and change his shape like the Homeric Proteus. A great lover of women, he used this ability to visit them at night, often using the shape of a heron. Always seen as a handsome warrior, he had a self-propelled ship called 'Wave Sweeper' and lived with his wife Fand* in *Tír Tairnigiri* ('the Land of Promise'). During a quarrel he left her unprotected against attacks by the Fomorians*. She summoned Cúchulainn* as her champion and they became lovers. Manannán had children by mortal women, including

Móngan*, and is the presiding deity of the Isle on Man, which is named after him. The frequent mists that cover the island are explained (by the Manx tourist board) as Manannán's making the island safe from invasion.

Medb (*anglice* Maeve) was originally a goddess but appears in mythology as the devious, acquisitive and much-married queen of Connacht, conferring the kingship on her spouses. She is chiefly associated with the epic *Táin Bó Cuailgne** (*The Cattle Spoil of Cooley*), which deals with the discovery that Finnbhenach*, the white bull, would not join the herd owned by a woman, and the herd of Ailill*, her husband, was thus greater than hers. She persuaded Ailill to lead with her an army that would secure the Donn Cuailgne*, the fabulous Brown Bull of Ulster. The war resulted in the death of many warriors, including Cúchulainn*, who confronted her armies alone because the Ulster warriors had been debilitated by the curse of Macha*. She was, in true goddess fashion, free with her sexual favours and was killed by a 'brain ball' from the sling of Forbaí, the son of her former husband, Conchobhar Mac Nessa*, while swimming in Loughrea.

Miach was the more-talented son of Dian Cecht*. He replaced the silver hand that his father had made for Nuada Airgetlámh* with one of flesh and blood and thus enabled him to recover the kingship of the Tuatha Dé Danaan*. He also managed transplants, once giving a human the eye of a cat. His father, jealous of his medical skill, attacked him three times but Miach was able to cure the wounds. He finally succumbed to a lesion in the brain. Even so, 365 herbs with the power of healing even mortal wounds grew out of his grave. These were gathered by his sister Airmid, who laid them out on her cloak in an order which indicated what each should be used for, but the relentless Dian Cecht scattered them so that no one knew which was which.

Midir was the son of the Dagda* and an important member of the Tuatha Dé Danaan*. He was the husband of Étain*, who suffered several metamorphoses at the hands of Fuamnach*, his first – and understandably jealous – wife. She became in turn a pool, a worm and a fly who was swallowed by the pregnant wife of the Ulster warrior Etar*. The child was a daughter, a second Étain, whom Midir tried to claim as his wife. He first tried to win her in a game of *fidchell** from her husband, Eochaidh Eireamh, and then abducted her, the two flying out of his chimney in the form of swans. He took her to his palace at Brí Leith near Ardagh in County Longford but eventually yielded her to Eochaidh, to whom she bore yet another Étain. When the Dagda relinquished his leadership of the gods, Midir refused to accept Bodb Dearg* as the new ruler. It was in the titanic war that followed that the Dé Danaan, torn apart by dissension, lost their divine power, literally went underground and were degraded into the fairies of later folklore.

Milesius (also Mil) was the father of the invaders who, identified with the historical Celts, constituted the final wave of incomers to Ireland. He was, according to tradition, of the thirty-fifth generation in a direct line from Adam and lived in Spain, as an alternative name for him, *Míle Easpain,* indicates. His son Ir (whose name must have played a part in the naming of the island) was lost in a storm raised by the Tuatha Dé Danaan* to prevent the Milesian invasion, and his wife, Scota (another significant name), died fighting them in Kerry. Milesius himself never reached Ireland, though in mythological and historical terms his invasion was the successful one. Bereft of leaders, the ordinary folk of the Dé Danaan became the servants of the sons of Mil, as the Fir Bolg* had earlier been enslaved by the Tuatha.

Mongán was the son of Manannán Mac Lir* and Caintigerna, a mortal queen of the land around Lough Neagh. When the child was three nights old, his father took him to his palace in the *Tír Tairnigiri* ('the Land of Promise') and invested him with much magic power. When he reached maturity he left his father's home and married the beautiful Dubh Lacha, his exact coeval. Later, in a burst of unreasonable generosity, he offered his friend Brandubh, King of Leinster, any wish that he had the power to grant. Brandubh, who had long desired Dubh Lacha, asked for her as his wife. Mongán could not in honour refuse but used his inherited powers to sleep with his wife in the guise of a monk and trick Brandubh into accepting a withered old hag, temporarily made very beautiful, in exchange for Dubh Lacha. He was eventually killed in battle but, as one story has it, returned to the land of men as Fionn Mac Cumhail*.

Mórrígán (also Mórrígú) was the chief goddess of war and slaughter and was synonymous with ghastliness in the Celtic pantheon. She favoured the form of a raven or crow, giving those birds a bad reputation. She was active on the side of the Tuatha Dé Danaan* in the battles of Magh Tuireadh* and had intercourse with the Dagda* astride a river. Her relentless animosity against Cúchulainn* was based on his sexual rejection of her, and when, in the form of a she-wolf, he managed to wound her, he realised that he would not survive. As he died, she perched in the form of crow on his shoulder and watched as a beaver lapped his blood.

Murna of the White Neck* was the descendant of Nuada* and Ethlinn* and the mother of Fionn Mac Cumhail*.

N

Naoise was the consort of Deirdre* and the eldest of
the three sons of Usna*. He and his brothers Ainlé*
and Ardan* were Red Branch knights* in the service
of Conchobhar Mac Nessa*. When he met Deirdre,
the betrothed of his master, she realised that he
fulfilled her criteria of male beauty; they fell in love
and fled to Glen Etive in Alba*. Returning home
under the parley of Fergus Mac Roth* – and against
Deirdre's advice – he and his brothers were killed by
the usual mixture of betrayal, magic and misdirected
loyalty. He was buried by a little lake opposite
Deirdre's grave and the branches of the pine trees that
grew out of their graves meshed to form a lovers' arch
like that of Baucis and Philemon.

Navan Fort (anglicised form of *An Eamhain*, the
modern Irish form of 'Emain Macha'*) is the impressive
hill fort with tumulus and enclosure two miles west
of Armagh City that is taken to be the site of the
mythical – and historical – centre of the Ulster kings.

Nemed was the leader of the third of the waves

of supposed invaders of the island of Ireland. He was a descendant of Japhet, the son of Noah, and arrived from Scythia with thirty-two ships. Many of the passengers died at sea of famine but, magically, when the survivors landed their numbers increased sufficiently to defeat the Fomorians* three times. After Nemed's death his followers became the Fomorians' slaves, however. An insurrection by Nemed's followers which included an attack on the Fomorian stronghold of Tory Island* was put down with great ruthlessness. Only 30 of the 16,000 followers of Nemed were left alive, and these few left to find a kinder shore.

Nessa was the mother of Conchobhar* by the druid Cathbad* while married to Fachtna, King of Ulster. On his death, his half-brother Fergus Mac Roth* acceded to the throne but in return for Nessa's sexual favours allowed Conchobhar to reign for a year. She advised her son so well about the duties of kingship that at the end of the year he was able to refuse to abdicate while retaining the full support of the people. Nessa's power gradually diminished as her son became the most famous of all the Ulster kings, the only serious blot on his character being his treatment of Deirdre* and the sons of Usna*.

Niamh is the name of several characters in Irish mythology, most notably Niamh Chinn Óir* ('of the golden head'), a daughter of Manannán Mac Lir and lover of Oisín*, a poet and the son of Fionn Mac Cumhail*. Niamh spirited Fionn away to her father's home, *Tír Tairngiri** ('the Land of Promise') to live there. After three weeks (300 years in the calendar of mortals) of idyllic happiness, during which, miraculously, a daughter, *Plúr na mBan* ('Flower of Women'), was born, Oisín pined for Ireland and the company of the *Fianna**; Niamh reluctantly permitted him to return, with dire results.

Nuada was known as *Argetlámh* ('silver-handed') and was the first leader of the Tuatha Dé Danaan* at the time of their 'taking' of Ireland but lost his hand at the first battle of Magh Tuireadh*, against the Firbolg*. This imperfection made it impossible for him to continue as the Dé Danaan's king, even though Dian Cecht* made him a serviceable hand of silver. When the latter's son Miach*, who had more medical skill than his father, created a hand of flesh for him, he was able to resume his position as king. In the second battle of Magh Tuireadh he and his wife Macha were slain by Balor*.

O

Ogma was the god of eloquence and literature, the son of the Dagda* and the husband of Étain, the daughter of Dian Cecht*. He was known as Ogmios to the Continental Celts and was celebrated in Ireland as the inventor of Ogam, the earliest form of writing in pre-Christian Ireland, which was generally non-literate . This form of writing consists of lines drawn above and below to meet or cross perpendicularly or diagonally a central base line. In the surviving examples the base line is usually the edge of a standing stone.

Oisín ('little deer'), who is known as Ossian in English literature, was the son of Fionn Mac Cumhail* and Sadb*, daughter of Bodb Dearg*. He was a leading warrior of the *Fianna** and a fine poet. He married a fair-haired stranger called Eibhir, and their son Oscar* was a significant hero in the latter days of the band. He was carried off by Niamh*, the daughter of

Manannán Mac Lir*, to her home in *Tír Tairnigiri* ('the Land of Promise')*. One version of the story maintains that his sojourn there lasted three weeks but Niamh had to advise him that this meant 300 mortal years. Nonetheless, in his time there she produced a daughter, known as *Plúr na mBan* ('the Flower of Women'). The story of his return on a magic horse and an accident with a broken stirrup that led to his touching the land of Ireland with his foot and becoming his mortal age comes from a later, Christian tradition. In this version, as an ancient over 300 years old, he tells St Patrick wondrous stories of the Fenian heroes, especially stories about his father and son and his cousin Diarmuid*. Oisín played a significant part in the story of Gráinne* in that it was he whom the reluctant betrothed of Fionn tried to seduce before persuading Diarmuid to elope with her.

Oscar: was the son of the poet Oisín* and the grandson of Fionn Mac Cumhail*. The *'os'* element of the name means 'deer' – a reminder of the story of his grandmother Sadb*. Though earlier noted for his clumsiness, he became a fearsome warrior, at times reaching the level of

Cúchulainn in battle-frenzy. He was, however, a noted peacemaker and, like Oisín, refused to carry out Fionn's vengeance on Diarmuid* and Gráinne*. He died in single combat at the last battle of the *Fianna** at Gabhra in County Dublin (the equivalent of Camlan in the Arthurian cycle), inflicting a mortal wound on his adversary Cairbre*, the high king who succeeded his father, Cormac Mac Art*, and was determined to break the power of his predecessor's armed force. Oscar's wife, Aidín*, died of grief and was buried on Beann Edair (Howth Head). **Otherworld**: the realm of the gods and the resting place of mortal souls before reincarnation. The place was visible only once a year, at Samhain*, the beginning of the Celtic winter season and now associated with Hallowe'en, when the powers of evil have licence before yielding to the sanctity of all the saints of heaven, an event which is still celebrated on 1 November. Aspects of the Otherworld are found in *Tír Tairnigiri**, *Tír na nÓg** and *Hy-Brasil**.

P

Partholón led the third invasion of Ireland. He, like Nemed* and Milesius* of Biblical ancestry, led his followers to occupy Munster, which was at the time occupied by Fomorians*. He is credited with introducing agriculture to Ireland, bringing with him ploughs and ploughmen. He and his followers were wiped out by plague. The elements of folk memory of actual colonisation are particularly obvious in this account.

R

The Red Branch Knights were the warriors who defended Ulster during the reign of Conchobhar Mac Nessa*. Cúchulainn* was their greatest champion. Members of the force began their training when they were seven years of age. Their headquarters was at Emain Macha*.

S

Sadb was the daughter of Bodb Dearg* and the mother of Oisín*. She had been turned into a deer by the Dark Druid* and would have been killed by Fionn Mac Cumhail* except that his hunting dogs would not go near her. (In one account Fionn, sensing her human elements, crushed his hound Bran* between his legs to prevent it attacking her.) That night she came to Fionn in human form and became his mistress, having discovered that the Dark Druid had no power within the *Fianna* compound. Later, when Fionn was off hunting, the Dark Druid turned her back into a fawn and she disappeared. Fionn searched for her for seven years and finally, at the foot of Ben Bulben in County Sligo, found a naked boy who had been raised as a deer. He recognised the boy as his son, calling him 'little deer'.

Samhain was the feast that marked the end of the agricultural year and the beginning of winter. It was held at the end of October, when the Otherworld* became visible to mortals and evil was allowed brief licence. Fires were extinguished and relit by druids and cattle were slaughtered and salted for winter feeding. In Christian times the feast became Hallowe'en, when the devil and his minions are allowed to wreak havoc before the feast of All Saints.

Sceolan was one of the hounds of Fionn Mac Cumhail*, Fionn's nephew and the twin brother of Bran*. The twins were born to Fionn's sister while she had been metamorphosed into a bitch.

Sétanta was the given name of Cúchulainn* before he became the Hound of Culann.

Sidhe are the hollow hills where the Tuatha Dé Danaan* went to live after their defeat by the sons of Mil*. There, after aeons, they became the people of the *sidhe*, the fairies of later folklore, appearing most notably in the form of a banshee (*bean-sí* in modern Irish), a fairy woman who appears to members of particular families with portents of death.

Suibhne Geilt was a king who, in the Christianised version of the myth, was cursed by St Ronán after the battle of Moira so that, although he retained his human form, he assumed the characteristics of a bird. The image of a man turning into a bird continues to fascinate modern Irish writers.

T

Tailtu was a Firbolg* princess who became foster-mother to Lugh Lámhfada* and gave her name to Tailtinn (Teltown), which is between Navan and Kells in County Meath. She wore herself out clearing the forests and making plains and was buried in the necropolis there. Mourning games were held in her honour at the beginning of August each year on her foster-child's orders. This event, Aonach Tailteann, later became incorporated in the festival of Lughnasa*, which marked the end of the summer season and initiated autumn.

Táin Bó Cuailgne (*The Cattle-Spoil of Cooley*) is the epic account of the struggle between Medb* of Connacht and Conchobhar Mac Nessa* over the matter of the Donn Cuailgne* ('the Brown Bull of Cooley'). This epic, like Homer's *Iliad*, with which it can be compared, is concerned with warriors, weapons and the involvement of deities in mortal affairs. It also gives a picture of Ireland many hundreds of years before the birth of Christ. Part of the Red Branch* or Ulster Cycle of tales, it is preserved in the eleventh-century *Lebor na hUidre* (*The Book of the Dun Cow*). Finnbhenach* ('the White-Horned Bull') refused to become part of a woman's herd and joined that of Aillil*, thus making his herd greater than that of his wife, Medb*. She mustered an army to carry off the Donn Cuailgne from County Louth. The Ulster territory was defended by Cúchulainn*, who was the only one of the Red Branch Knights* unaffected by the curse of Macha*. The epic ends with a battle between the two bulls which the Donn wins, carrying the carcass of Finnbhenach on his horns on a rampage through the centre of Ireland until he too drops dead.

Tara (Temair) is the ancient site in County Meath that is regarded as having been the residence of the high kings of Ireland and the headquarters of the *Fianna** during the reign of Cormac Mac Art*.

Tír na mBan ('the Land of Women') was a place of beautiful women of the Otherworld*. It was usually visited by voyagers on *immrama**, where all earthly wishes are fulfilled. Inevitably the visitors grow tired of all the entertainment provided and begin to long for home.

Tír na nÓg ('the Land of the Young') is the Irish Valhalla or Olympus, where gods and mortals remain eternally young and live in perfect amity.

Tír Tairnigiri ('the Land of Promise') is a paradisal island that was the home of Manannán Mac Lir* and his daughter Niamh*.

Tory Island is an island off Donegal that was the home of the Fomorians*, especially Balor of the Evil Eye*, who imprisoned his daughter Ethlinn* in a glass tower on Tor Mór, a headland to the east of the island.

Tuatha Dé Danaan are the old gods of Ireland. They came on the fifth wave of colonists, enslaved the native, menial *Firbolg** and carried on murderous wars of attrition with the Fomorians*, who were the quintessence of evil. They were descendants of the mother goddess Dana* and, though normally genial and aesthetically inclined, were not without mortal failings, including cupidity, jealousy, envy and lust. The Christian scribes who recorded their epic adventures sanitised them somewhat, denying their deity – since there was only one true God – and rendering them as heroes and heroines but allowing them some residual magic. They were defeated by the last wave of invaders, the sons of Milesius*, and went underground into the *sidhe** assigned to each by the Dagda*. There they continued to live as the *Aes Sidhe**, becoming in time *Na Daoine Beaga* ('the wee folk'), the fairies of later folklore whose possible malevolence had to be countered.

U

Usna was the husband of Ebhla, the daughter of the druid Cathbad* and the granddaughter of Aonghus Óg*, the love god. Their three sons, Naoise*, Ainlé* and Ardan*, figure in the story of Deirdre*, the eldest as her lover and the others as companions and bodyguards during their sojourn in Alba*. They were tricked into returning to Ireland and were killed on the orders of Conchobhar Mac Nessa*.

Select Bibliography

Berresford Ellis, P. *A Dictionary of Irish Mythology*. London, 1987.

Colum, P. *A Treasury of Irish Folklore*. New York, 1963.

Dillon, M. *Irish Sagas*. Cork, 1968.

Gregory, Lady Augusta. *Cuchulain of Muirthemne*. London, 1902

———. *Gods and Fighting Men*. London, 1904.

Heaney, M. *Over Nine Waves*. London, 1994.

Joyce, P. W. *Old Celtic Romances*. London 1907.

Kennedy, P. *Legendary Fictions of the Irish Celts*. London, 1891.

Mac Cana, P. *Celtic Mythology*. London, 1970.

Matthews, J. & C. *The Aquarian Guide to British and Irish Mythology*. Wellingborough, 1988.

Ó Dónaill, N. *Seanchas na Féinne*. Dublin, 1942.

O'Faolain, E. *Irish Sagas and Folktales*. London, 1954.

O'Sullivan, S. *Folktales of Ireland*. London, 1966.

Stewart R. J. *Celtic Gods, Celtic Goddesses*. London, 1990.

Sykes, E. *Who's Who in Non-Classical Mythology*. London, 1993.